WELCOME TO THE WORLD OF
Octopuses

Diane Swanson

Whitecap Books
Vancouver / Toronto

Edited by Elizabeth McLean
Cover design by Steve Penner
Interior design by Margaret Ng
Typeset by Susan Greenshields
Photo credits: James A. Cosgrove iv, 4, 10, 12, 14, 18, 26; David Doubilet/First Light 2; George Grall/First Light 6; Neil G. McDaniel 8; James B. Wood 16, 22; David Hamilton 20; Seattle Aquarium 24

The author gratefully acknowledges Jim Cosgrove of the Royal British Columbia Museum for reviewing this manuscript.

Printed and bound in Canada

Canadian Cataloguing in Publication Data

Swanson, Diane, 1944–
    Welcome to the world of octopuses

    Includes index.
    ISBN 1-55285-023-4

    1. Octopus—Juvenile literature. I. Title.
QL430.3.O2S92 2000   j594'.56   C00-910077-6

For more information on this series and other Whitecap Books titles, visit our web site at www.whitecap.ca

The publisher acknowledges the support of the Canada Council for the Arts and the Cultural Services Branch of the Government of British Columbia for our publishing program. We acknowledge the financial support of the Government of Canada through the Book Industry Development Program for our publishing activities.

Contents

World of Difference

AN OCTOPUS IS MOSTLY ARMS. And what wonderful arms they are! All eight of them can stretch, twist, and bend without having any joints. Along these arms sit rows of suckers—dozens or even hundreds—depending on the age and kind of octopus. The suckers work independently, gripping objects such as small stones and fine wires.

The octopus has a soft body with no bones. It doesn't even have a shell, although its ancestors once did. Its only hard part, a strong parrotlike beak, is surrounded by its eight arms.

The giant Pacific octopus is one kind of cold-sea octopus that might live over four years.

1

The headlike mantle of the octopus is a bag of skin and muscle. It keeps the brain and other important organs under cover. The mantle also contains glands that secrete slime onto its skin. Wearing a slimy coat protects an octopus from infection and helps it slide easily through small openings.

No one knows how many different kinds of octopuses

As an octopus swims, it shoots water out of the short, hoselike funnel above its arms.

exist, but at least 60 kinds live around North America. Worldwide, there are probably over 150. Some are shorter than a paper clip, but others stretch the length of three doors or more.

An octopus has no ears, so it depends on its other sense organs. Its arms—especially its suckers—are used for touching, smelling, and tasting. And its eyes can see as well as yours. Peeking over rocks is easy for an octopus because it can raise its eyes above its mantle.

MOVING RIGHT ALONG

Reach, anchor, and p-u-l-l. Using all the suckers on its long arms, an octopus crawls quickly and effortlessly across the sea floor.

When it swims, the octopus sucks water into its mantle and fires it out through its funnel. That jets the animal backward, and all its eight arms trail behind. It can easily shift direction by pointing its funnel different ways. If it wants to swim slowly, the octopus simply squirts out water with much less force.

Where in the World

OCTOPUSES HANG OUT IN SALTY SEAS. Some live in tidepools or in shallow water close to shore. Others stay in deep water—more than 3 kilometres (2 miles) down. There they feel and smell their way through the dark. Some kinds of octopuses range between shallow and deep water.

When an octopus is not out searching for food, it's usually snuggling inside one of its dens. Caves or holes in undersea rocks, and nooks and crannies in sunken ships make good octopus homes. So do roomy shells and castoff pails and cans. Sometimes an octopus builds a den out of piles of

Luckily for this octopus, it found a hiding place beneath a rocky outcrop.

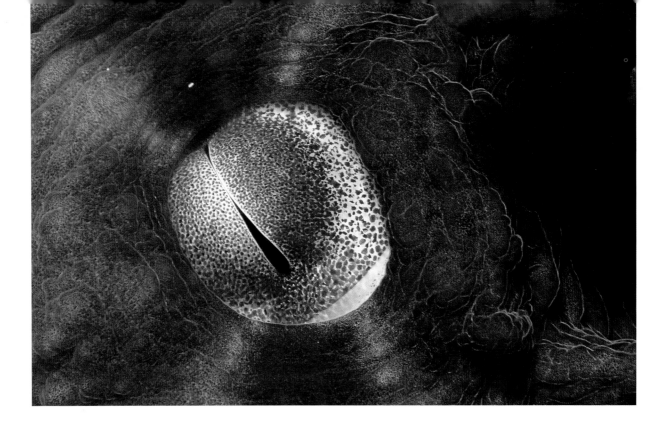

An octopus views its world through narrow slits—its pupils.

stones, shells, and bottle caps. Or it might use these items to narrow or hide the entrance to its den.

Even a large octopus needs only a small doorway. Its soft body can squeeze through almost any opening wide enough for its beak.

An octopus lives all on its own, but it

often has several dens. It might use one at each end of its hunting range and others in between for protection while eating. Some dens are used again and again by generations of octopuses; others are used only once.

Nearly every ocean in the world is home to some kinds of octopuses, but warm waters have more variety. Off the coasts of North America, octopuses have been found living in the Pacific Ocean, Atlantic Ocean, and Gulf of Mexico.

It's not easy to watch an octopus. It tends to watch right back—and it usually tries to hide. Besides, divers aren't able to stay underwater for long periods.

Researchers might attach a special tag to an octopus, so they can track its movements by radio from a boat or satellite. Or they might use a camera on an ROV (Remotely Operated Vehicle) to follow an octopus day and night. Once it gets used to the camera, the octopus doesn't seem bothered by it.

World Full of Food

CRABS, SCALLOPS, SNAILS, FISH. They're just some of the animals an octopus eats. Like you, it dines on its favorite foods, but a big octopus might also grab seabirds—even smaller octopuses—if it has a chance.

When it spies lunch, an octopus sneaks in close. Then it leaps. It traps its prey in a pocket of water under its webbed arms. Next, it releases a toxin from its glands into the pocket, stunning its victim.

Sometimes an octopus pokes the tips of its arms into cracks and holes—sniffing, tasting, and feeling for food. When it finds

Working its way across the sea floor, an octopus is on the hunt.

A pile of shells—
mostly from crabs—
is all that remains of
an octopus feast.

something, the octopus yanks the prey out, stuns it, and tucks it under its arms. Before heading back to its den to eat, the octopus might gather a dozen or more crabs or other small prey.

Safe at home, the octopus can use its tough beak to rip into the prey, biting or tearing off chunks of food. It can also scrape its food, using a tongue covered with thousands of tiny, horny teeth. This tongue is always replacing old worn teeth with new sharp ones.

The octopus also uses its toothy tongue to drill a hole through the thick shells of animals such as clams. It injects chemicals that turn the soft insides to mush, then it sucks or scrapes them out with its tongue. Leftovers are pushed outside. A growing pile of empty shells can show divers the location of an octopus den.

It can be hard to keep an octopus at home. One aquarium store owner discovered that his octopus gobbled up some of his fish at night. Alone in the store, it climbed out of its tank and entered the tanks of its neighbors. The octopus usually sneaked back before morning, but sometimes it hid in other parts of the store.

A big octopus might even be able to escape from a covered tank. It can raise a lid weighed down by several cinder blocks.

World of Words

THE SILENT OCTOPUS TALKS WITH ITS SKIN. It might say, "I'm mad," by raising the skin above its eyes to make a pair of "horns." But mostly, an octopus speaks by changing color. In its skin are stretchy cells, each filled with a colored chemical that may be red, orange, yellow, or black. The octopus widens or narrows the openings in these cells, exposing more or less of each color. It can even display different combinations of colors.

Many kinds of octopuses can make patterns—including streaks, stripes, and blotches—on different parts of their

This ruby octopus is saying something in body language, but scientists aren't sure just what.

13

"Horns" of skin rising on this octopus show that it's angry.

bodies. Several also have layers of cells that reflect the colors of nearby objects.

Before male octopuses mate, they often change colors, sometimes producing stripes. That's how they tell other males to get lost. By turning a pale gray or white, many octopuses show they're frightened. A dark red might mean they're angry or excited.

Skin colors and their meanings vary with the kind of octopus. Some kinds might say, "I'm content," through a patchwork of soft colors; others, by turning a dark red.

All octopuses can talk fast. In fact, few other animals can change color as quickly. Octopuses take just a fraction of a second to open or close their color cells completely. They can run through a number of different combinations and patterns so fast the human eye can barely follow.

There's a mystery about the octopus. It changes color to talk—and to blend with its surroundings—but it can't see in color.

That doesn't matter to the skin cells that reflect colors of objects the octopus passes. And that doesn't affect the thin skin of small octopuses that lets colors show right through. But most of the octopus's amazing shades and patterns are controlled by nerves from its brain—and these nerves are triggered by what the octopus sees!

15

Dangerous World

The color and pose of this white-spotted octopus might scare away its enemies.

PLENTY OF PREDATORS EAT OCTOPUS MEAT. People, dolphins, seals, sea lions—even fish, such as halibut and cod—all hunt for octopuses. So it's a good thing these eight-armed sea creatures have several escape tricks.

Frightened by the sight of a large predator—or a boat—an octopus might try to surprise its enemy. It might suddenly change color, flatten its body, and curl its arms in toward its mantle. Some octopuses also develop dark circles around their eyes.

Next, the octopus will likely shoot ink and mucus into the water. All octopuses

17

Firing brown ink
into the sea helps
this little octopus
escape from a
diver.

have glands that produce dark brown or black ink. (At one time, people used it for writing.) When the ink mixes with the water, it makes a dark cloud that confuses predators. Like a screen, the ink can hide the octopus for a few seconds, and it might dull an enemy's sense of smell. If once isn't enough, some octopuses can fire ink as many as six times in a minute.

Once predators lose track of the octopus, it has a chance to jet away, firing water forcefully out of its funnel. As it swims, it quickly changes the colors and textures of its skin, blending with its surroundings.

The octopus swims until it finds a safe hiding place. Then it squeezes through a crack in the rocks or swoops into a small den to take cover. Some small octopuses might hide under the sand on the sea floor.

UNARMING AN OCTOPUS

Half out of the water, an octopus clings tightly to a rock. A large bald eagle is trying to yank it off. Tugging at one arm, the eagle skilfully avoids the grasp of the octopus. But after a 10-minute battle, the bird leaves to find easier prey.

Like the eagle, other predators may try to rip an arm off an octopus. Luckily, that's something the octopus can lose without dying. In fact, it can grow a whole new arm, which might even branch into several small arms at its tip!

New World

MANY OCTOPUSES MAKE GOOD MOTHERS. A female searches for a safe den to use as a nursery. She might even close off the entrance by building a stone wall. Then she gets busy laying her eggs — from hundreds to more than a hundred thousand of them. They've already been fertilized by a male octopus. Using a specially designed arm, he placed a package of sperm into the female's mantle.

Using her own mucus, the mother sticks the eggs in strands to the wall or ceiling of her den. Then she nestles close to them, where she stays day and night. She rarely —

Mom on guard! Protecting her eggs is a full-time job for this octopus.

21

See-through eggs make it possible to spot these tiny octopuses before they hatch.

if ever—eats while she guards her eggs. The octopus pushes away intruders, such as snails, sea stars, crabs, and fish, which might eat her brood. To provide oxygen to the eggs, she sprays them with water from her funnel.

In cold waters, a mother's care can continue for over six months. But in warm seas, young octopuses often burst out of their eggs much sooner. As they hatch, their mother showers them with water. That helps them jiggle free of the eggs.

The new arrivals look just like tiny adult octopuses. They can change color, produce ink, and shoot water from their funnels. Predators gobble up most of the hatchlings right away. Some of the survivors—depending on the kind of octopus—drift and feed at the water's surface before heading for the sea floor.

No wonder octopuses surprise people. They do the most amazing things!

- Armstrong would be a good name for an octopus. It can move objects heavier than itself.
- Of all the spineless animals in the world, the octopus is the brainiest. It's about as smart as a cat.
- An octopus owns three hearts—two to pump blood through its gills and one to pump blood around its body.

Fun World

IT TAKES BRAINS TO HAVE FUN. And like cats and dogs, an octopus seems to be smart enough to play. After all, it can figure out how to get a crab out of a jar—even if it has never seen a jar before. The octopus might first try to grab the crab through the glass. But soon, it figures out how to unscrew the lid or pull out the cork to reach its prey. If another octopus is nearby, it can learn to do the same thing more easily— just by watching the first octopus.

In experiments, octopuses have learned to pick out objects of different shapes and sizes. When they're rewarded with food for

What a ball! An octopus checks out new objects and seems to play with some of them.

some choices and punished with mild electric shocks for others, they learn quickly. The octopuses remember their lessons quite well, too. They get better and faster with practice.

No one knows what games an octopus plays in the wild, but in an aquarium, it seems to have fun with a toy. When researchers dropped an empty pill bottle into a tank, the

Divers might all look the same to you, but an octopus can learn to tell them apart.

octopuses tasted it—in case it was food. Then some of them ignored the bottle, while others used it to play games. Squirting water from their funnels, they moved it along to the rear of the tank. A current carried it back, and they squirted the bottle away again. One octopus made the bottle circle the tank over and over. The games lasted from 10 to 30 minutes. What seemed odd was that no octopus used any of its amazing arms to bat the bottle around.

GETTING TO KNOW YOU

An octopus can have fun with people. In an aquarium, it might squirt water at a familiar face or climb to the top of its tank to "greet" someone. Even in the sea, an octopus easily recognizes people it knows—in spite of their masks and all the other diving gear they wear.

Touch an octopus arm and that arm might touch you right back. As it feels around, its strong suckers might nuzzle your fingers. They can sometimes pull a watch or ring right off!

Index